Translated works of Baudelaire, Verlaine, Rimbaud et. al, and Selected Poems

S. D. Metcalfe

First published 2019 by
C.L. Wriggs Publishing House
Sydney, Australia

Translations from French

Childhood
 - Arthur Rimbaud

The Death of Lovers
 - Charles Baudelaire

The Noise of the Cabarets, the
Filth of the Gutter
 - Paul Verlaine

Correspondences
 - Charles Baudelaire

Harmony of Evening
 - Charles Baudelaire

To Julie
 - Alfred De Musset

Selected Poems

Into the Sky

Through Windows of Eyes

Marine Depths

The Lion [*Française*]

The Lion [*trans.*]

De Ravageur [*Française*]

De Ravageur [*trans.*]

Silence Marring Absence of Heart

Days of Existence

Childhood [*excerpt*]

- A Rimbaud

I

...

By the ribbon of the
forest - the flowers of
dream tinkle, burst, and
have electrical clarity, -
the girl whose lips are
orange, her knees
crossed in the clear
deafening deluge,
penumbra of nudity,
transversed in
accoutrement by
rainbows of sky, the
flora, the sea.

...

II

Magical flowers were chanting. The embankment cradled him. The beasts of fabulous elegance circulated about. Clouds amassed over a sea of haughtiness formed by an eternity of warm tears.

III

In the woods there is a bird, whose song arrests you and makes you blush.

There is a clock that does not sound.

There is a pothole with one nest of white animals.

There is a cathedral which descends and a lake that rises.

There is a small car abandoned in the undergrowth, or which descends the common lane, forming ribbons.

There is a troop of little entertainers in costume, glimpsed from the road one travels along, beyond the edge of the woods.

There is, finally, when famished and in thirst, someone who chases you.

...

V

   At an enormous distance of weight above my subterranean lounge room, the houses implant themselves, the brown mist assembles. The quagmires are either red or black. Township of monstrosity, night without end!
   Not as high up there are sewers. By its sides there is nothing but the impassiveness of the globe. Perhaps chasms of azure, mineshafts of fire.

Perhaps it is on these
levels the reconnoiter of
moons and comets, of
seas and fable.

In the hours of
bitternesses I imagine
balls of sapphire, of
metal. I am a master of
silence. What is it that
appears in the basement
window blenching the
corner of my vault?

The Death of Lovers

- C Baudelaire

We will have beds full of soft
perfumes,
The couches profound like a tomb,
And those strange flowers on the
mantelpiece
Unfold for us beneath the sky
which is more-beautiful.

Utilizing the struggle of their
warm fading embers,
Our two hearts will be two vast
flames
Which reflect their double
luminescence
In our two spirits, these mirrors of
same.

An evening ripening with the rose
and the blue mystique,
We exchange a lightning that is
unique
Like one long sob, integrally-
charged with our own goodbyes;

And much later an Angel entering
through doorways;
Reanimates vigorously, faithful and
joyous,
The terminal mirrors and the
deathful flames.

The Noise of the Cabarets, the Filth of the Gutter

- P Verlaine

The noise of the cabarets, the filth
of the gutter,
The plane trees that shed leafy-
effluence into black air,
The omnibus- a devastation of
recycled iron and mud,
Which grinds unhealthily upon
four tyres
As it's green and red eyes roll in
languor-
The workers going together to the
club, flouting the smoke from
Their pipes into noses of
plainclothes police,
Roofs dripping moisture, walls of
algae, pavements that glisten,

Bitumen deformed, brooks filling
with sewer,
Ah! There is my route - at the end
is where paradise lies.

Correspondences

- C Baudelaire

Our Nature is a temple where
vibrant pillars
Leave on occasion confused
sentences;
The man traverses through forests
of symbols
Who are watching him with eyes
of familiarity.

As long echoes merge into the
distance
in one dark and profound unity,
As vast as the night and it's clarity,
The scents, the colours and the
sounds respond with refrain.

It is the fresh perfume of infants'
flesh,
Sweet like an oboe, green as fields
of grass
- and the others, corrupted, rich
and triumphant,

In accordance with the expansion
of infinite things,
Such as amber, musk, benzoin and
incense-
Which sing the transcendence of
one's spirit and senses.

Harmony of Evening

- C Baudelaire

Here is the time when trembling
on the stem
Each petal evaporates within its
own censure;
The sounds and the perfume make
currents of evening air;
Waltz melancholic and languorous
vertigo!

Each petal evaporates within its
own censure;
The violin shuddering like an
afflicted heart;
 Waltz melancholic and languorous
vertigo!

The sky is sad and beautiful like a
grand repository of religious
intent.

The violin shuddering like an
afflicted heart;
A tender heart, that hates the
eternal vast nothing of darkness!
The sky is sad and beautiful like a
grand repository of religious
intent.
The sun has drowned in its own
blood that has frozen.

A tender heart, that hates the
eternal vast nothing of darkness,
The passage of light collects the
last traces!
The sun has drowned in its own
blood that has frozen...
Your memory shines within me
like an ostensible horror!

To Julie [*trans.*]

- A De Musset

They demand of me, on the streets,
To know why I look stunned
gawking at tall chicks,
Making fumes from my cigar in the
sun,
And why did I pass my youth
In three recent years of idleness,
And how I traversed so many
nights without sleep?

Give to me those lips, Julie;
Those nights of folly which made
you pallid
Have left your coral jewels lucid.
Perfume the harmony of your
breath;
Give to me, my African,
Your luscious lips of pure blood.

My publisher cries at the top of his
lungs
That his machine is forever
prepared
and that mine, however, cannot.
Those of the honest gentry, whom
the club admires,
Have not yet deemed themselves
ready to pronounce
That I will not reinvigorate and
convalesce.

Julie, do you have any of that wine
from Spain?
For yesterday we made battles
whilst on campaign;
Can you see any remnants more?
Your mouth is scalding, Julie;
Therefore invent for us some kind
of folly
Where we may find perdition for
the soul and body.

One says the gourmande within me
has rent,
That nothing remains of my
stomach,
That I have become just frightful
bits;
It is my contention that it were
worth the sorrow
To convey me to Saint Helene,
with this malady left inside my
heart.

Come, Julie, you must attend–
To see me some day burned up into
cinders
Like Hercules on his outlook of
rock.
Since it is along with you I must
expire,
Open that robe, Dejanire,
So that I may rise upon your
burning pyre!

Scene Set to Music

- A Rimbaud

By the place tallied into mean
lawns,
Square and all correct; the trees
and the flowers,
And all the bourgeoisie puff;
strangled by the heatwave and
Bringing, each Thursday evening,
their obsequious jealousies.

- The military orchestra, in the
midst of the garden,
Balance their shaking-sticks at the
'*Valse des fifres:*'
- Surrounding the premier ranks,
the dandy parades;
The notary dangles like a charm
from his own brooch.

The men who eye their incomes
draw attention to the hiccups,
The fat office morons trailing their
fat women,
Closely by whom, like unofficial
maids,
Flounce voluminous
feathers taking on the
air of advertisement.

On benches green, the
club for retired
shopkeepers
Poke critically at the
sand with their
pommelled canes,
Heavily serious
discussing the trade
agreements;
And then, taking a silver
snuffbox, they resume:
"In summary!..."

Elephantine fat
spreading over the
bench, and in rolls of the
kidney,
One bourgeoisie with
bright buttons, a
paunchy Dutchman,
Savors his Onnaing
brand whereby shreds of
tobacco
Dishevel - you can tell
an article of contraband;
-

The long green turf
ricochets with the
leering of thugs,
And, rendered romantic
by the singing of the
trombones,

Very naive and
diminutive footsoldiers,
fuming at roses
Caress the babies to
enjoin their nannies...

- Me, I follow, shabby
like a student,
Beneath green chestnut
trees the more-alert
girls:
Who, saliently aware;
turn radiantly
To me, their eyes
brimming with things of
indiscretion.

I dare not say one word:
I admire constantly
The skin of their creamy
white necks embroidered
by locks of wild hair:

I am, beneath the
corsage and the fragile
attire,
The divine small of her
back beyond the
curvature of shoulders.

Soon I have hunted-
down her boots, the
stockings...
- I re-construe their
bodies, scorched by
beautiful fevers.
To them I am ridiculous
and they talk about me
in low voices...
- As my desires brutally stitch
themselves onto their lips.

Dream for Winter

- A Rimbaud

In the winter, we shall leave
in a little pink wagon
    Where the cushions are
    blue.
We will be very comfortable.
Nests of kisses there lie in
bizarre repose
    at warm corners,
    mollified.

You must shut tightly your
eyes, so as not to see, through
the glass,
    Grimaces of shadows in
    the growing dark.
These monstrosities snarling,
the populace
    Of demons black and
    wolves black.

And then the sensation upon
your cheek...
One small kiss, like a harmless
arachnid
    It scurries across your
    neck...

And to me you say: "Look for
it!" inclining your head,
- And we'll take our time to
find that small beast,
    Who is an excellent
    journeyman.

The Ship [*excerpt*]

- E Signoret

The ship is perfumed with coronas
of roses,
Whose flanks of cedar are
resplendent with sun.
A wave that vaguely glistens
faraway from the morose shores...
On the terrain and on the sea it is
midday.

Above the forests of brilliant
emerald elms and above the sands
It is midday! The vessel creaks and
trembles in the winds
And the man reaches out his arms
to an imperishable sky-
The earth is vividly alive, the sky is
vividly alive!

They stretch out a sail of gold,
whose shadow even possesses a
radiance.
'The anchors we curved from the
iron of coutres,
That old wind furrows in the
fullness of sail;
We carried away whole springs.'
...
The sun sank.
...
The pilot alone views Diana's
resplendent clarity,
Whose pretty carriage renders
guidance through nocturnal airs
And stretches above them a torch
of exhilarated palpitation;
The crew sleep on as they float
upon the sea.

Moesta et Errabunda

- C Baudelaire

Tell me- does your heart seldomly
involute, Agathe,
Far distant from the black ocean of
the putrid city,
To another ocean where splendor
brilliantly expurgates,
Blue, clear, profound, like
virginity?
Tell me- does your heart seldomly
involute, Agathe?

The sea, the vast sea, console us for
our labors!
What demon endowed the sea, that
racque chanteuse,
With an immense accompaniment
of organ fabricated from the wind's
rumbling,

Whose only function is to produce
this sublime lullaby?
The sea, the vast sea, console us for
our labors!

Transport me, carriage! Deliver
me, frigate!
Far away! far away! here the mud is
formed by our tears!
- Is it true that, seldomly, the sad
heart of Agathe
gives up a secret: far from remorse,
crimes, dolor,
Transport me, carriage... deliver
me, frigate?

As you are so entirely-faraway,
paradisiacal perfume,
Where beneath a clear azure all is
with love and joy,
Where everything one loves is
worth the dignity of being loved,

Where in the pure voluptuousness
one's heart drowns!
As you are so entirely-faraway,
paradisiacal perfume!

But the green paradise of childhood
loves,
The courses, the songs, the kisses,
the bouquets,
The violins vibrating behind the
knoll,
With braces of wine, the eve
filtering groves,
- But the green paradise of
childhood loves

That innocent paradise, ripened by
pleasures of the furtive,
Could it really be further away
than India and China?
Perhaps we may recall its physical
presence with plaintive cries

And enliven once more the voice of quicksilver,
The innocent paradise, ripened pleasures of the furtive?

The Albatross

- C Baudelaire

Often for amusement the
men of the crew
Capture the albatross,
vast birds of sea,
Indolent companions to
their voyage, whose
aloofness surveys their
Navigations that slither
over a repugnance of
abysms.

Sorrowfully deposed-of
onto the deck;
These kings of the
azure, ashamed of their
awkwardness,

Languish piteously
whilst the once eloquent
and magnificent white
wings
Trail at their sides like
oars used for rowing.

This voyager of the air;
how goofy it has
become, and crippled!
Previously handsome,
now it is comical and
vulgar.
One sailor irritates his
beak with a pipe
And another, limping,
mimes the infirmity of
one who once soared!

The poet is the
resemblance of this, our
prince of clouds

Who haunted the
tempest evading the
archer;

Exiled upon the soil to
an underworld of
ridicule,
Whose giant wings
impede marching.

Romance [*excerpt*]

- A Rimbaud

I

You aren't really serious, when you
are seventeen.
- One beautiful twilight, filled with
beer and lemonade,
And boisterous cafe-bars lustered
by the light of their own
illuminated clarity!
- You go amongst the greenery of
lime trees on the promenade.

The lime trees are scented-well on
this good evening of summer.
The air sometimes is so sweet, that
on the edges of your eyelids,
The wind ruptures into sound, -
the town is not that far away, -

Perfumes of the vine and perfumes
of beer...

II

- There, you see an aperture, a
small piece of chiffon
Somber blue, encased by one little
branch,
pricked by a star of misfortune,
that fades
with soft shivering, tiny and
completely white...

Into the Sky

and up there you have it: joyous
shooting into the sky,
the path of some rocket, traversing
clouds, abode *généreux*

uniting in magnificent clarity
the scent of flowered water splayed
from an innocent wrist
and the thoughtful dalliance of
childhood games
lifted up from the pavement, and
cleansed far from here.

such blueness bedazzles the
ordinary eyes, far more than
sublime treasures...
here, count amongst these
recompense
the luscious green scenery that
sprouts from your tongue

and blooms in cold fire, which
shelters and sustains the innocence
of hope.

when the raindrops fall your mind
is brought up, up
        and up:
there, you have it!

through windows of eyes
comes the real thread of seasons:
I adore the flames

that were placed there delicately,
from fingertips,
where nobody could locate their
source of fuel...

weeping, the scattered febrile
petals
of a large blue moon are my pilot
lunar-
this quietude of silver light
wends to the darkness subtly
a blueness of void.

Marine Depths

With tiny mouths leaving bubbles
of air
& their decided motions cleaving
torrentous fare,
With nought but their faith to hide
them

The poor little fishes, awash in
their wishes;
They have no mother to guide
them.
Upon them do angels stare
Or does one dream a countenance
to bide them?

They steal and allow sleep's
notional escape;
Deceived upon a yoke of mire,

Cleansed alone with their coldness
a'fire,
Seeking to hold onto strange
desires:

Wisdom in the subtle array
Of fins and eyes and suffering
decay...
Littering their atmosphere with
discarded instances
     of hunger
What angel pauses amongst them-
their fears to
     stay-
& makes with happy joy their
lonely thoughts allay?

The Lion [*Française*]

le berger ne se doute pas un lion
qui attend sans demande
ils sont les fruits goûter repas.
il est le chien qui contamine les
graminées.

au sein de la froideur céleste le ciel
de la nuit aliène et pourtantil
est de la même bouquet de chair
qu'ils aspirent.

The Lion [*trans.*]

it is the shepherd who suspects the
lion
both of whom await without
request
the fruits of a good repast.
it is the dog that contaminates the
grasses.

within the cold celestial sky
the night alienates and yet
it is the same bouquet of flesh to
which they all aspire.

De Ravageur [*Française*]

La folie j'admire. il détruit, absous
de ses propres
      flammes
énigmes de l'inimitié. la laideur je
veux baiser.

Lorsque les pertes de l'éloquence
sont tout
      simplement
une annotation de culpabilité se
sont abstenus:

Je vous blâme pour mon
désenchantement
      douloureux.
sous cette ville, les égouts suivent
passages anciens,
dans l'obscurité chante le fétide.

De Ravageur [*trans.*]

Madness I admire. it destroys,
absolved of its own
     flames
the enigmas of enmity. the ugliness
I want to kiss.

Where eloquent losses are simply
an annotation of absent culpability:

I blame you for my disenchantment
of sorrow.
beneath the city the sewers follow
ancient passages,
in obscurity chants the fetid.

Silence Marring Absence of Heart

Silence marring the absence of my
heart, grow
        fonder-
in your requiem beneath time, with
resoundment,

for I call to you... enfolded. how is
it
you are there in another moment,
sustained?

if it were memory of tomorrow's
declinations
of cartographic photographic
within my world of worlds; then

touching the sun in one breath of
humility,

inside many days and nights,
there is an oxygen clear: of so
many stars.

Graveyard Shift

Cigarettes can fix you together: for
to fear the
smoothness of cardboard whisper
dry recollections across your hands
is to turn into the heart a
monotony of stone.

How sad, the hollow eyes of ironic,
Inhabiting these concrete halls
mechanic.
They touch nothing without
bitterness or pain.

days of existence
fell into the distance
like the forgotten friends you
meant to call
but thought were lost-

months on end found them again
in one desultory room after
another;
where in the dense solitude
the days blurred...

I said to myself,
'Joy is the saddest burden of all'.

The Shooting Star

this star came out
it was a shooting star tracing
against the shadows of the sky
a garland crochet spiderweb
gossamer
could not be more delicate than the
morning
traced across a right brow

gone so quietly and without
monument,
who could say it ever was there?

Spring Haiku-Twin

of icewater shock
one remains gasping for breath
undone we must be/unable to
breathe

An Ode to the Country - Eustice Miller.

- written for A Heyward, aged 11.

O to be, and to decree:

'Here I am,'mongst fair
hills of the country,
O this lovely country
that I see' —

whereupon
the hillocks gently
grazing cattle, sheep,
and the occasional equine,
pause to seek your eye
as the car of your passage
passes by...

And to further remark

along the traverse of their
boundary (as they attend
to their continual grazing)

'These clouds do you see them,
coming as they do over yonder?
With their billowing majesty, so
amazing- making me wonder!'

Such speech may
prompt within one a
joy of certain kind,
that begins within
the chime of peaceful delight:
such a vast, open space and road
unfurling,
'neath a sky filled with thunderous
clouds and rainbows!-

receive this joyous spark, it is the
tinder that doth ignite
the mind!

O the country, the fair,
lovely country,
where I might take leave
of my senses and worries
to walk amidst colourful
petals of wildflowers
that upon my approach
quiver and flutter away;
secret butterflies.

O to travel! and to admire
distances perhaps we once
had not thought-of to aspire:

to chance beyond your
window pane a single
glance of towns that
are at once both new and
unfamiliar–

save the sign which
lieth at the outskirts

that gives to you a name
for places one mightn't even
remember.

Perhaps along the way
you are tired in the car,
sometimes your armpits pong,
sometimes you and your sister
do not get along-
going slowly, often stopping, esp.
when the traffic is disgruntled;
you can start to feel a bit skitty...
thankful though, even then,
to be heading far away from the
city where the edges of sky
(unlike in the metropolis)
are often clear, seldom gritty.

Upon the morn, eventime,
or any time betwixt:
in the country the
view is always very, very pretty.

In the country the air
is so fresh and clean
that the breath one gathers is
nothing short of supreme-
the sky one doth admire
from vantage that shall not require
a single thing more
than the habit of a slight upward
tilt of the neck to acquire.

Stars are always beautiful, even
when barely visible,
but in the country they illuminate
the sky:
woven into distant grains of
nocturnal light
O how lovely, lonely and
glistening is the country night!

And,

How nice it is, in the country;

your soul's peaceful purveyor.
Such inspiring creeds are
from the country bred,
whose relaxing credence
inspires you once more
at night in your bed,
and as your drive about the
aforementioned, oft-maligned,
country.

How might one loosen
such an emotion and
bear yet refrain,
for the grey and the dark
of soft falling rain;
how to explain the rawness,
the ruggedness,
fair semblances of beauty-
the pastures green, vast,
ambiguously unctuous-

and lovely, yes, always so lovely–
so gentle, rolling, seemingly
endlessly lovely...
Of the verdant, relentless,
undulating country?

Perhaps, on your travels,
you take a book to read,
or follow your traverse
as you advance upon the map;
entertain yourself by creating
anagrams from the license
plates of passing cars:
or lean against a pillow formed
from your rolled-up jumper
pensive whilst your vehicle is
gliding,
giving way to a languorous
slumber or happy respite:
a nap, what delight!

Often, upon a trip unto the
country,
you come to stop at a station to
allow the refuelling of your car.
When someone goes inside the
store to buy petrol,
they might return with sweets, or
other similarly delectable items to
eat:
the possibility of the many varied
combinations of candy, a promise
of flavoursome riot
that's delicious if taken carefully
(although with too much of
there is no diet).

And if you stop at a cafe in the
country just to dine,
you shall hear often a familiar
refrain (and then, at that, all the
time)

'Your prices so cheap!
Your cakes so (as the French
would say) 'exquisite'!'

which is a marvelous thing to say
even without rhyme-
but when applied to one's lips is
almost divine!

You could have vanilla-iced coffees,
and
double-chocolated mud cake all
topped0
with white chocolate and sugared
raspberries
all served with real freshly-
whipped cream;
the same to have also with the
triple berry compote cheesecake;
and ice cream with the cheesecake,
or cherry and custard apple
strudel...

so many yummy things that in
the country are served,
you will be stuffed, kit and
caboodle.

Now, in the country, as you
enact your motion,
to complete his and her vocation
you will see humankind
merging with nature-
around you liest much that is
food...

(although to consume right there
would be considered rude)

For the living beings are still
getting ready for us to eat;
they are yet to be packaged
and prepared so we can
swallow then excrete.
Along the way to becoming

your next meal,
they all must grow,
and live, and feel!

Like potatoes. And beetroot. And
cabbages, ribs, oranges and lime,
and herbs and carrots and cherries,
chicken and sausages. And limes.
(And where a warmth of the
tropical favours the clime:
bannanas and pineapple.)

So many things; so many
numerous, interesting, thought-
provoking things
people grow for us to eat
in the country:
hard it is to count in all of one's
head exactly how many...

And always, as you look out
through your window

traversing the road that can be so
slow and meandering/winding
(so patiently, utterly winding)
the view of the country is
forever pretty.

Of the city there are certain things-
many amusing and quaint.
But few of these compare
to the pleasure of vaulting a gate,
and, following the rise of a carpet
of grass patterned with the yellow
of weed-flowers and the hum of
roving bees,
finding a meadow's stream that
flows through the contours of the
earth:

a vein caused by rain, from
when'er the clouds from the sea
draw close unto the country's
altitude

and shed of themselves a little, so
they might rise once more,
whitened...

leaving behind a remnant, a
collation of their tears, a moving
fissure!
Who could have guessed
that beside the road,
o'er a gate, so near,
the gushing of a pure stream,
heavenly tinkle to my ear?

Past the modern brilliance of
industry,
So many secrets that liest in the
country beyond the city-
whereupon the morn, eventime and
times in betwixt-
that goddamn view is always so
very pretty.

O to be, and to decree,
'Fair hills of the country:
How doth I admire and amuse my
senses
by drinking such sweet and
fragrant future-remembrances'
Exuberant, to be sure, my heart for
ever more,
bequeathed with the knowledge of
the clean, wholesome and honest
goodness of the country,
whose beneficial clime pertains to
me, and unto my heart:
a ceaseless, pedant, magnanimous,
effrontery-

Oh! How we all must love
the dear and lovely country!

Printed in Great Britain
by Amazon